You Are a Gift!

SHELLY MORROW WHITENBURG
ILLUSTRATED BY AUDREY GILLIES

REDEMPTION PRESS

"Every good and perfect gift is from above."
James 1:17 NIV

Published by Redemption Press, PO Box 427, Enumclaw, WA 98022

Toll-Free (844) 2REDEEM (273-3336)

Redemption Press is honored to present this title In partnership with the author. The views expressed or implied in this work are those of the author. Redemption Press provides our imprint seal representing design excellence, creative content, and high quality production.

Illustrations © 2021 by Smiling Sticks, LLC

ISBN 13: 978-1-64645-172-2

Library of Congress Catalog Card Number: 2020918708

To all children...
You are most precious and
are such a gift to life!

You are a gift!
You've been one from the start.
For the gift inside you
Came from God's loving heart!

No matter the path,
No matter the way,
You're here to help brighten
Each and every day!

God's heart is love

And it's meant to shine!

It lives in your life

And it lives in mine!

This gift overflows
With amazing love!

It's awesome
and wonderful.

It's from
Heaven above!

God's love is so big!
It's meant to be shared.

You can do this anywhere!

How do you share
A gift so dear?
Just live from your heart
Each day of the year!

So be patient and kind.

Be helpful and share.

Be polite and welcoming.
Show that you care!

Smile and hug.

Lend a helping hand.

Invite and include.

Spread love throughout the land!

Treat others well.
It will come back to you.
This rule is golden
And so very true.

So keep it up
And keep it going!

As you share,
Love keeps on growing!

Moving on and on,
Endlessly around.

Love is the gift
That cannot be bound!

Every day
Help spirits to lift.
It's easy to do
Because you are a gift!

Order Information

To order additional copies of this book, please visit
www.redemption-press.com.
Also available on Amazon.com and BarnesandNoble.com
Or by calling toll-free 1-844-2REDEEM.

CPSIA information can be obtained
at www.ICGtesting.com
Printed in the USA
LVHW072150110321
681233LV00001B/29